BLACK AMERICANS
IN SCIENCE
AND ENGINEERING

CONTRIBUTORS OF PAST AND PRESENT

ILLUSTRATED AND EDITED BY

Eugene Winslow

Afro-Am Publishing Company, Inc.
A Division of African American Images
Chicago, Illinois

Introduction

Throughout the history of the United States, many African Americans have made significant contributions to technology. These contributions have helped make life better, safer and more pleasant for all Americans.

The automatic traffic signal, the first American-made clock, electric light filaments, train car couplers and the automatic shoe making machine are among the early inventions of African Americans. Toward the end of the 19th century Elijah McCoy invented a device for automatic oiling of factory machinery. It contributed so much to industry it became known as the "real McCoy," an expression still used to denote genuine quality.

We hope you enjoy reading about Elijah McCoy and the other African American inventors, scientists and engineers depicted in this booklet. We also hope they may inspire you to consider science and engineering in your career plans. If you like science and math, and are willing to work hard at your studies, you can find a rewarding career through engineering. Talk with your teachers and counselors about science and engineering.

Table of Contents

Benjamin Banneker

(1731-1806)

Benjamin Banneker was an inventor, a mathematician, an astronomer, a surveyor, and an essayist. As an inventor, he built a wooden clock which kept accurate time until he died in 1802 at the age of 75. This homemade clock is believed to have been the first clock totally built in America. Born free in Ellicott, Maryland, Banneker was a self-taught man who used his mathematical skills to develop and publish a widely-used almanac which was issued each year from 1792 to 1806. He spent many nights studying the stars in order to make his almanac as accurate as possible. As a surveyor, he helped lay out the streets and buildings of Washington, D. C. And as an essayist, he wrote about the evils of slavery.

James Forten

(1766-1842)

James Forten invented a device which made it easier to handle the large heavy sails of the big ships that sailed the seas before the days of the steamship. As a boy he loved to go down to the docks along the Delaware River and watch the ships maneuver up to the pier to unload their cargo. He noticed how important the expert handling of the sails was in guiding the ships. At the age of eight he began working in a Philadelphia sail loft with his father, and some thirty years later bought the sailmaking shop from the owner. During this time he not only invented and perfected his device, but also learned all about the sailmaking business. Due partly to his invention, his sail loft became one of the most prosperous in the city.

Jan Ernst Matzeliger

(1852-1889)

J. E. MATZELIGER
LASTING MACHINE
No. 274,207.   PATENTED MAR. 20, 1883

Up in Lynn, Massachusetts, near Boston, people in the shoe business laughed at 25-year-old Jan Ernst Matzeliger when word got out that this former sailor was secretly working on a machine that could automatically make shoes, back in the 1870's. After all, the best brains in the shoe business had invested thousands of dollars trying to develop such a machine, and they had failed. "Couldn't be done," they said, as they continued to make only from 40 to 50 pairs of shoes per day, by hand. Finally, Jan, who was good at mechanical things decided he had developed the kind of machine needed—a machine that could make thousands of pairs of shoes in a day. In 1883, over ten years after he had started developing his shoe machine, Matzeliger was granted a patent on it.

3

Norbert Rillieux

(1806-1894)

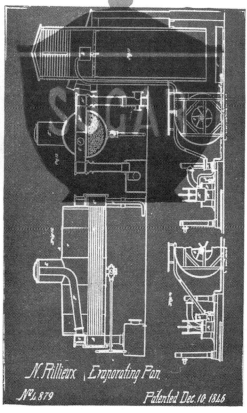

N. Rillieux Evaporating Pan.

Nᵒ 4,879   *Patented Dec. 10. 1846*

An engineer, Norbert Rillieux patented a sugar-refining process in 1846 which revolutionized this industry. Son of a slave mother and of the master of the plantation where he was born in New Orleans, Louisiana, in 1806, Rillieux was educated in France. He also taught school there at the age of 24 years. The sugar-refining process he developed greatly reduced the cost of producing good sugar from sugar cane and from the sugar beet. He also published papers on the uses of steam and on the steam engine. In 1854, because of discrimination in Louisiana, he left that state for good, returning to France where he again turned to engineering inventions.

Granville T. Woods

(1856-1910)

Patents for over 35 electrical inventions were granted Granville T. Woods, of Columbus, Ohio. Many of this electrical engineer's inventions were sold to General Electric, Westinghouse, and the Bell Telephone Companies. While Woods, who was born in Columbus, Ohio, April 23, 1856, invented more than a dozen devices to improve electric railway cars, and many more for controlling the flow of electricity, his most noted invention was a system for letting the engineer of a train know how close his train was to others. This device helped to cut down accidents and collisions between trains. Among his other top inventions were a steam boiler furnace and an automatic air brake used to slow or stop trains.

Elijah McCoy

(1843-1929)

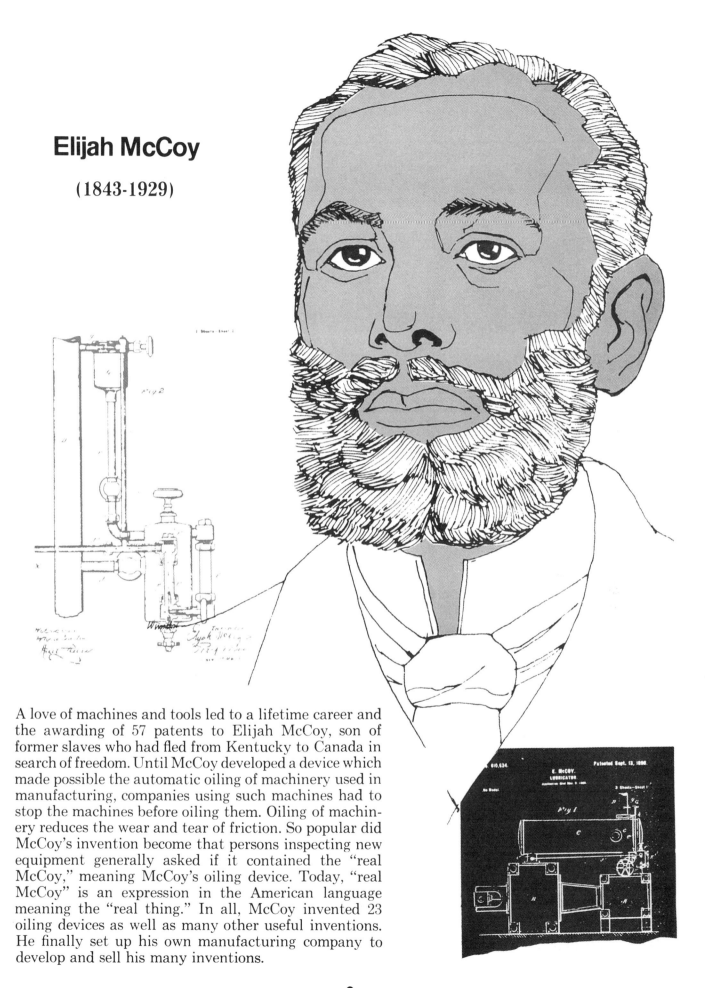

A love of machines and tools led to a lifetime career and the awarding of 57 patents to Elijah McCoy, son of former slaves who had fled from Kentucky to Canada in search of freedom. Until McCoy developed a device which made possible the automatic oiling of machinery used in manufacturing, companies using such machines had to stop the machines before oiling them. Oiling of machinery reduces the wear and tear of friction. So popular did McCoy's invention become that persons inspecting new equipment generally asked if it contained the "real McCoy," meaning McCoy's oiling device. Today, "real McCoy" is an expression in the American language meaning the "real thing." In all, McCoy invented 23 oiling devices as well as many other useful inventions. He finally set up his own manufacturing company to develop and sell his many inventions.

Andrew Beard

(1849?-1921)

Andrew Beard was born a slave on a plantation in Alabama. Before he became an inventor he was a farmer, carpenter, blacksmith, a railroad worker, and a businessman. In 1892 he patented his first invention, a special kind of engine. It was while working in the railroad yards that he got his idea for a device which would automatically hook railroad cars together. This device was patented in 1897, and became known as the "Jenny Coupler." It eliminated the dangerous job of hooking railroad cars together by hand, and probably saved thousands of lives and limbs of railroad workers. He improved this device in 1899, and later received $50,000 for its patent rights.

Garrett A. Morgan

(1875-1963)

Garrett A. Morgan was a prize-winning inventor who developed a safety helmet breathing device widely used by firemen in many American cities in the early 1900's. His invention became popular after he and his brother used it to rescue over two dozen men who were trapped under Lake Erie, at Cleveland, Ohio, when an explosion occurred in a tunnel which was under construction. He was awarded a gold medal by the City of Cleveland for his heroic rescue. He later received a gold medal at the Second International Exposition of Safety and Sanitation, in New York, in 1914. Morgan is best remembered for his invention of the automatic stop sign. This invention, now called the traffic or "stop light," controls the flow of vehicles through street intersections.

Lewis H. Latimer

(1848-1928)

Son of a runaway slave, Lewis Howard Latimer became an electrical engineer who worked for Thomas A. Edison, inventor of the light bulb, and Alexander Graham Bell, inventor of the telephone. Many of Latimer's ideas, including the fine carbon wire which lights up, went into Edison's light bulb. Latimer was the only African American, and one of the original 28 persons who formed the "Edison Pioneers," a group dedicated to keeping alive Edison's ideals. The Edison General Electric Company, for which Latimer worked, in 1892, merged with a second firm and the new company became the present General Electric Company. Latimer was also a noted patent expert, draftsman, author, poet and musician.

George Washington Carver

(1864-1943)

Probably the best known African American scientist and inventor is George Washington Carver, who alone, nearly revolutionized agriculture in the South. At a time when the South's major crop-cotton-was faced with total destruction by the boll weevil beetle, Dr. Carver, through scientific experiments showed the South that peanuts, soybeans and sweet potatoes (yams), among other crops, should be planted, along with cotton. Thus, if one crop failed, there would be others from which farmers could make money. Known as "The Wizard of Tuskegee," Dr. Carver developed hundreds of products from the peanut, the soybean, the pecan nut, the sweet potato, and even from weeds. Today, there are many schools and other institutions named in memory of Dr. Carver.

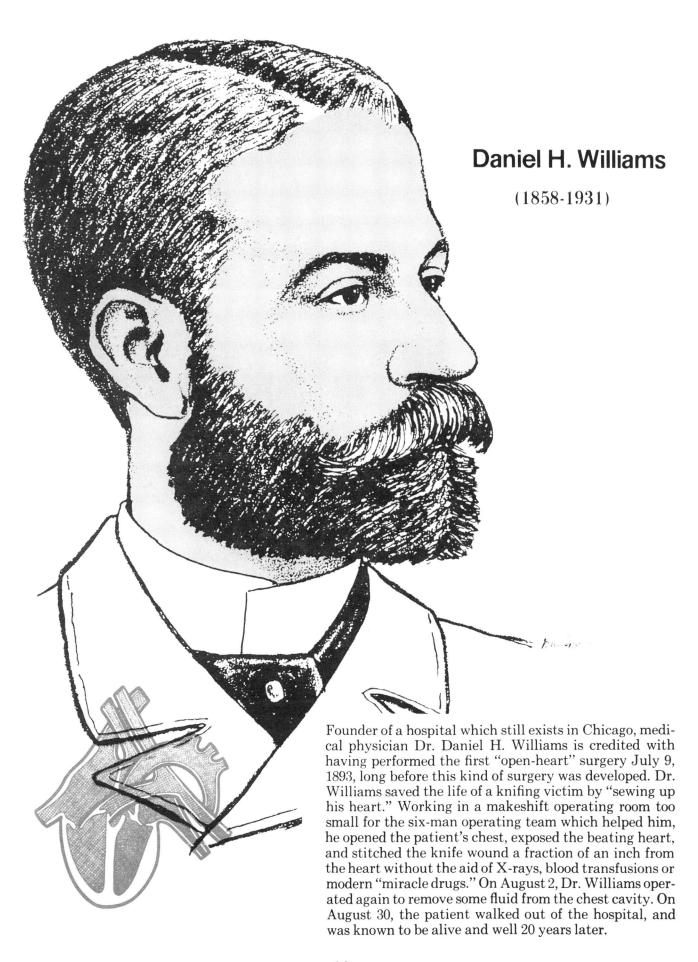

Daniel H. Williams

(1858-1931)

Founder of a hospital which still exists in Chicago, medical physician Dr. Daniel H. Williams is credited with having performed the first "open-heart" surgery July 9, 1893, long before this kind of surgery was developed. Dr. Williams saved the life of a knifing victim by "sewing up his heart." Working in a makeshift operating room too small for the six-man operating team which helped him, he opened the patient's chest, exposed the beating heart, and stitched the knife wound a fraction of an inch from the heart without the aid of X-rays, blood transfusions or modern "miracle drugs." On August 2, Dr. Williams operated again to remove some fluid from the chest cavity. On August 30, the patient walked out of the hospital, and was known to be alive and well 20 years later.

H. C. Webb

(1864- ?)

H.C. Webb invented a machine which cleared away palmettos, an unwanted kind of growth found in the farm fields of the southeastern region of the United States. The device looked something like a three-wheeled plow, and was pulled by a thirty-horsepower engine. It helped farmers to clear away as much unwanted growth in one day as it normally took ten men 10 days to clear away-about ten acres. The Webb Palmetto Grubbing Machine was patented in 1917. Webb also invented a barrel stave machine and a special kind of drill press but lost the rights to them because he did not have them patented. But, during this period, hundreds of other African American inventors developed labor-saving devices for which they did not receive government patents.

Frederick M. Jones

(1893-1961)

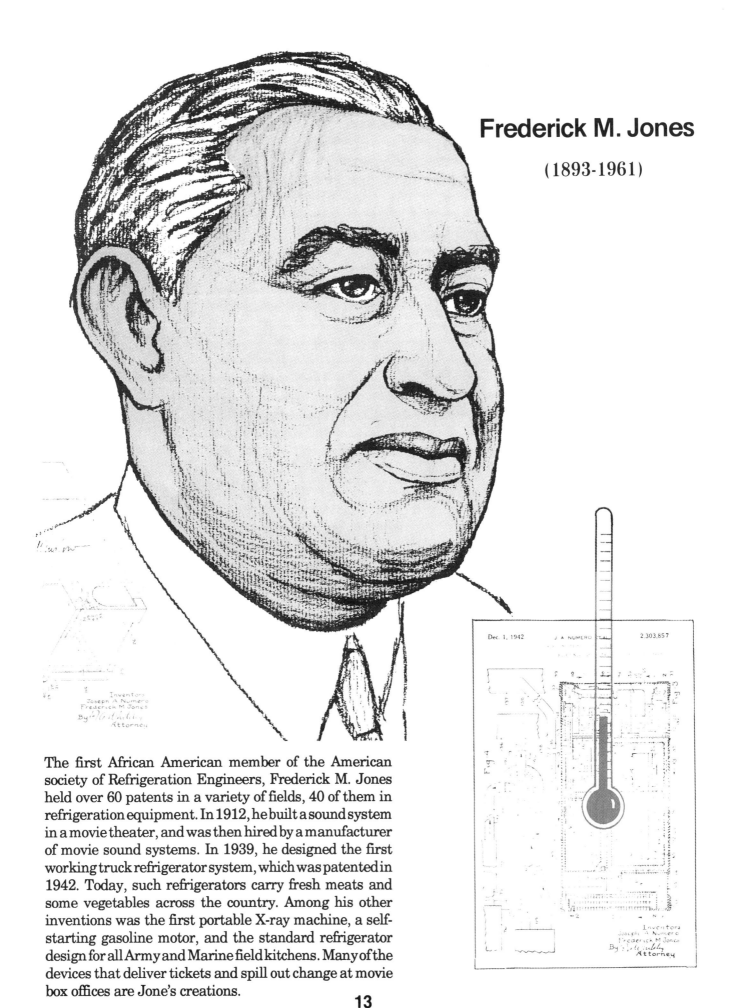

The first African American member of the American society of Refrigeration Engineers, Frederick M. Jones held over 60 patents in a variety of fields, 40 of them in refrigeration equipment. In 1912, he built a sound system in a movie theater, and was then hired by a manufacturer of movie sound systems. In 1939, he designed the first working truck refrigerator system, which was patented in 1942. Today, such refrigerators carry fresh meats and some vegetables across the country. Among his other inventions was the first portable X-ray machine, a self-starting gasoline motor, and the standard refrigerator design for all Army and Marine field kitchens. Many of the devices that deliver tickets and spill out change at movie box offices are Jone's creations.

13

Charles H. Turner

(1867-1923)

Common honeybee, *Apis mellifera*
A. Queen; B. Worker; C. Drone

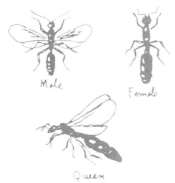

BLACK ANTS

Male

Female

Queen

Charles H. Turner, who obtained a Ph.D. degree from the University of Chicago in 1907, was noted for his knowledge of ants and bees. He originated a way of watching and recording the habits of insects and small animals, the ways they act toward one another, and the way they reacted to things that happened to them. A type of behavior in insects is now called "Turner's circling" after his detailed description. Through forty-seven research papers which he published between 1892 and 1923, he showed how humans were a lot like animals and insects, and helped the world better understand why man acts the way he does.

Madame C. J. Walker

(1869-1919)

Before her invention, African American women had to straighten their hair by placing the hair on a flat surface and then pressing it with a clothing iron. After her invention was introduced, Sarah Breedlove Walker, who was known as Madame C.J. Walker, became one of the first American women of any race to become a millionaire through her own efforts. Madame Walker invented a hair softener and a special hair-straightening comb. Before her death in 1919, Madame Walker could count over 2,000 agents who sold her ever-growing line of Walker products and demonstrated the "Walker System" of treating hair. Her efforts laid the foundation for the cosmetics industry among African Americans.

Ernest E. Just

(1883-1941)

An outstanding research biologist, Dr. Ernest E. Just devoted a lifetime of study to the structure and function of the cell (cytology), the smallest unit of the body. His studies included how eggs are fertilized, how babies are born, and how the cells of animals function. In 1915, he won the Spingarn Medal, the highest award given by the NAACP to the person having done the most during the year to advance the process of African American people. He wrote two major books and more than sixty scientific papers in his field. His book, *The Biology of the Cell Surface,* which was used in many colleges, represented his lifetime of research, and was published in 1939, just two years before he died.

16

Louis T. Wright

(1891-1952)

A physician and surgeon, Dr. Louis T. Wright originated a method of operating on fractures about the knee joint, a brace for fractures of the spine, and a vaccination against smallpox, and supervised the first test of a miracle drug (aureomycin) on humans. He also advanced a new theory on the treatment of skull fractures and engaged in early cancer research. Graduating with highest honors from the Harvard Medical School in 1915, he was commissioned a 1st Lieutenant in the Medical Section of the Officers Reserve Corps in 1917, and rose to the rank of Lieutenant Colonel in the U.S. Army during World War I. In 1919, he became the first African American to be appointed to a New York City Municipal Hospital (Harlem Hospital) where he helped lower the death rate and increase the professional standards.

William A. Hinton

(1883-1959)

A specialist in the study and development of medicines to fight diseases, Dr. William A. Hinton is best known for the Hinton-Davies test used to detect the venereal disease, syphilis. In 1936, he wrote a text book on his studies, and became recognized as one of the worlds foremost authorities on the diagnosis and treatment of syphilis. Only three years after getting his doctor's degree from Harvard Medical School in 1912, he was made an instructor in preventive medicine and hygiene at this famous university. It is said that he could have made a fortune in private practice, but he chose to serve humanity by working in the field of public health.

Percy Julian

(1898-1975)

Finding a remedy for arthritis led to fame and fortune for Dr. Percy Julian, a noted chemical scientist. But, more important was the fact that his discovery made the medicine for this painful disease available to everyone at a much more reasonable price. Dr. Julian developed a way of making the medicine from the inexpensive American soybean instead of from the costly ingredient found in certain parts of animals and produced in Europe. At one time, he was president of two companies which he formed to produce this medicine. He later sold one of the companies to a leading medicine-making (pharmaceutical) firm for several million dollars.

19

Theodore K. Lawless

(1892-1971)

The skin, magnified many times

Dr. Theodore K. Lawless was a skin specialist (dermatologist) who became a millionaire from his studies, practice and development of medicines. He also contributed to the better understanding of syphilis, a venereal disease; and leprosy, a disease which wastes away the muscles of the body. Setting up his offices in the heart of Chicago's black community, he established one of the largest and best known skin clinics in the city. For many years, men, women and children, both black and white, crowded his waiting room from morning until night. But he still found time to teach at Northwestern University, work with the staff of Chicago's Provident Hospital, and share his knowledge with other doctors. In 1954, he was awarded the NAACP's Spingarn Medal.

Lawless Chapel, Dillard University, N.O., La

Charles W. Buggs

(1906-1991)

A scientists and educator, Dr. Charles Buggs, of Brunswick, Georgia, conducted special research on why some bacteria (germs) do not react to certain medicines. In several articles, he presented his ideas on penicillin and skin grafting, and the value of chemicals in treating bone fractures. In 1944, he contributed some of the results of his research to the world through twelve studies he helped to write. Three years later he wrote an important article on how to use germ-killing chemicals (antibiotics) to prevent and cure certain diseases. He also taught college biology, and made studies and suggestions on premedical education for African Americans. Dr. Buggs' research and teaching contributed to a better understanding of health and of the human body.

21

Charles R. Drew

(1904-1950)

The storing of human blood until it is needed to save someone's life was the major contribution of Dr. Charles Drew to science and medicine. He researched the nature of human blood and created what has become known as "blood banks," places where blood is kept in a special form (plasma) until needed by injured patients. In 1940, during World War II, the British asked Dr. Drew to establish a blood bank program for their country. After the war, he was appointed the first director of the American Red Cross Blood Bank, supplying plasma to the United States armed forces. He also became recognized as an outstanding surgeon, teacher and public servant, and in 1944 was awarded the Spingarn Medal.

Meredith Gourdine

(1929-   )

Head of his own manufacturing firm in New Jersey, Meredith Gourdine, an engineering scientist, found a way to make high-voltage electricity from gas. He and the other engineers in his company believe there are many uses for this discovery in our everyday life. Some of them are: refrigeration for preserving foods, supplying cheap power for heat and light in homes, burning coal more efficiently, making sea water drinkable by taking the salt out of it, making painting and coating processes easier, and reducing the amount of pollutants in smoke. His company has already made an exhaust purifying device for automobiles, devices for measuring air pollution, and generators for power stations.

23

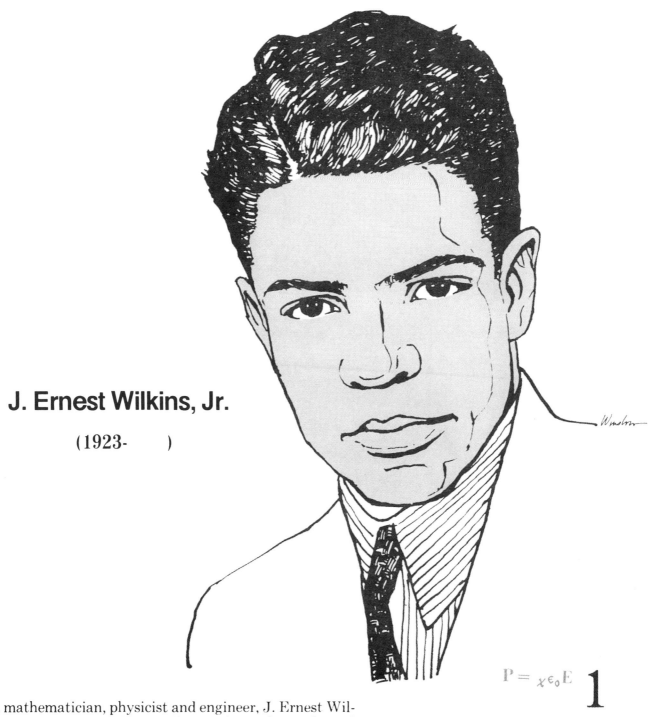

J. Ernest Wilkins, Jr.

(1923-)

A mathematician, physicist and engineer, J. Ernest Wilkins, Jr. contributed his skills mainly to the study and development of atomic power. As a teenager, Wilkins attracted nationwide attention when he finished college at 17, earned his masters degree one year later, and received his doctorate degree from the University of Chicago at the age of 19. For a time, he taught college mathematics, and later worked in the University of Chicago's metallurgical laboratory. As a relatively young man of 23, he was supplying the mathematical formulas for the production of special space-probing telescopes. By the time he was 27 he was part-owner of a firm which designed and developed nuclear reactors for creating atomic power.

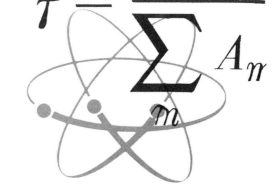

$$P = \chi \epsilon_0 E$$

$$\tau = \frac{1}{\sum_m A_n}$$

24

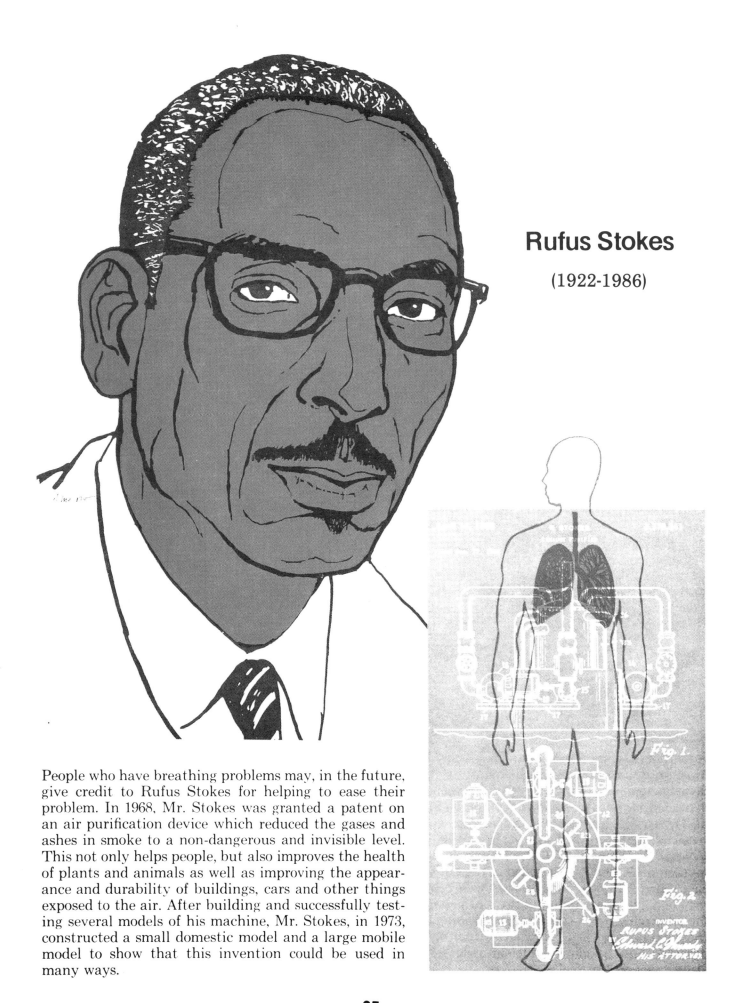

Rufus Stokes

(1922-1986)

People who have breathing problems may, in the future, give credit to Rufus Stokes for helping to ease their problem. In 1968, Mr. Stokes was granted a patent on an air purification device which reduced the gases and ashes in smoke to a non-dangerous and invisible level. This not only helps people, but also improves the health of plants and animals as well as improving the appearance and durability of buildings, cars and other things exposed to the air. After building and successfully testing several models of his machine, Mr. Stokes, in 1973, constructed a small domestic model and a large mobile model to show that this invention could be used in many ways.

Otis Boykin

(1920-1982)

An electronic scientist and inventor, Otis Boykin devised the control unit used in artificial heart stimulators, invented a variable resistor device used in many guided missiles, small components such as thick-film resistors used in IBM computers, and many other devices including a burglar-proof cash register and a chemical air filter. Starting as an assistant in a laboratory testing airplane automatic controls, Boykin was soon developing a type of resistor now used in many computers, radios, television sets and other electronically controlled devices. Many products made from his discoveries are manufactured in Paris and throughout Western Europe. One of his products was approved for use in military hardware for the Common Market.

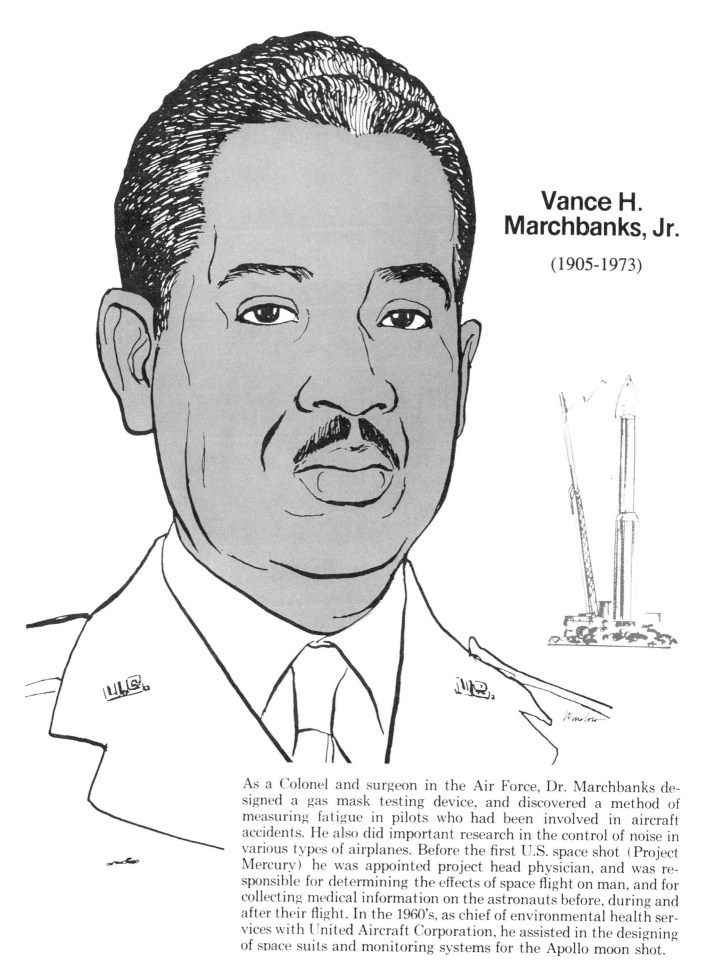

Vance H. Marchbanks, Jr.

(1905-1973)

As a Colonel and surgeon in the Air Force, Dr. Marchbanks designed a gas mask testing device, and discovered a method of measuring fatigue in pilots who had been involved in aircraft accidents. He also did important research in the control of noise in various types of airplanes. Before the first U.S. space shot (Project Mercury) he was appointed project head physician, and was responsible for determining the effects of space flight on man, and for collecting medical information on the astronauts before, during and after their flight. In the 1960's, as chief of environmental health services with United Aircraft Corporation, he assisted in the designing of space suits and monitoring systems for the Apollo moon shot.

John B. Christian

(1927-   )

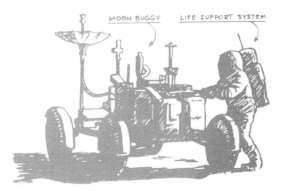

As a materials research engineer for the Air Force, John Christian developed and patented a variety of revolutionary lubricants that saved pilots' lives in combat and contributed to the success of the astronaut's mission on the moon. The lubricants, resembling cake frosting more than oil, could withstand temperatires ranging from minus 50° to 600°. In Vietnam, when the helicopters' oil lines were punctured by ground fire, the "soap" lubricants enabled them to return to their base. They were also used in the astronaut's back-pack life support systems, without which there could have been no moon landing, and were used in the four-wheel drive of the "moon buggy" making it possible to extend their moon exploration by 36 hours.

George R. Carruthers

(1940-)

Astro-physicist Dr. George Carruthers was the principal scientist responsible for the development of a special camera that made the trip to the moon aboard the Apollo 16 in 1972. Called the "far-ultraviolet camera/spectograph," the 50-pound, gold-plated unit was designed to study the earth's upper atmosphere and other interplanetary conditions. More than 200 frames of pictures were made of eleven selected targets. In 1973, another model of the camera was made for the Skylab 4 to take pictures of a comet speeding toward the sun. Carruthers was interested in science as a child and built his own telescope at the age of ten. From the age of 25, he made significant contributions to the field of electronic imaging and space astronomy.